Compliments of:

The Institute for Entrepreneurial Excellence
*The Power to Prosper*ˢᴹ

University of Pittsburgh | Joseph M. Katz Graduate School of Business
1800 Wesley W. Posvar Hall | 230 South Bouquet Street |Pittsburgh, PA 15260
Phone 412-648-1544 | Fax-412-648-1636
www.entrepreneur.pitt.edu

THE INSTITUTE FOR
ENTREPRENEURIAL
EXCELLENCE

THE POWER TO PROSPER

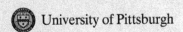 University of Pittsburgh

Values-Based
LEADERSHIP

*A Revolutionary Approach
to Business Success
and Personal Prosperity*

Values–Based LEADERSHIP

A Revolutionary Approach to Business Success and Personal Prosperity

Kenneth Majer, Ph.D.

MajerCommunications
a division of MajerStrategies, Inc.
San Diego, California

VALUES-BASED LEADERSHIP
A Revolutionary Approach to Business Success and Personal Prosperity

by Kenneth Majer, Ph.D.

MajerCommunications

Published by:
MajerCommunications
a division of MajerStrategies, Inc.
3655 Nobel Drive, Suite 160
San Diego, California 92122-1004
www.majervalues.com

Copyright©2004 by Kenneth Majer

Publisher's Cataloging-in-Publication
(Provided by Quality Books, Inc.)

Majer, Kenneth S.
 Values-based leadership : a revolutionary approach to business success and personal prosperity / Kenneth Majer.
 p. cm.
 ISBN 0-9743940-0-9

 1. Business ethics. 2. Leadership—Moral and ethical aspects.
3. Industrial management—Moral and ethical aspects. 4. Success in business. 5. Self-actualization (Psychology) I. Title.

HF5387.M35 2004   174'.4
                        QBI33-1552

Edited by Gail M. Kearns,
GMK Editorial & Writing Services, Santa Barbara, California

Book and jacket design by Peri Poloni,
Knockout Books, Placerville, California

Book production coordinated by
To Press and Beyond, Santa Barbara, California

Printed in the United States of America

What Business Leaders Are Saying About
Values-Based Leadership

A wonderful story about putting values to work. Values-Based Leadership will open your eyes to the benefits of ethics in business.

KEN BLANCHARD, co-author of *The One Minute Manager®* and *Full Steam Ahead!*

❧

A "can't-put-it-down" read that I finished in one sitting cover to cover! A very fulfilling way for values-based leadership to reach the business executive.

CARTER McCLELLAND, President, Banc of America Securities and former President, Deutche Bank USA

❧

It is a real rarity to pick up a business book and read it from cover to cover in one sitting, but that's what happened when I became so completely absorbed in reading Values-Based Leadership. *Engaging, lively and a clear demonstration of how a group of individuals can become a team through shared production and ownership of their central values!*

CURTIS W. COOK, Dean and Professor of Management, School of Business Administration, University of San Diego

❧

High marks for an excellent read on the importance of values presented in a very interesting fashion!

JERRY GOLDRESS, Turnaround Specialist and CEO of 102 companies

❧

This book is a "must read" for busy executives in achieving their vision of future success.

DONALD L. VERBICK, President, Delve Energy Group, LLC

❧

Today's frantic pace requires the successful leader to make periodic journeys back to fundamentals. One evening of "can't-put-the-book-down" intensity "woke me up" and "kept me up!" Values-Based Leadership gave me the practical tools to reshape our company's culture.

DONIELLE SULLIVAN, Chief Operating Officer, Radiology Service Partners, LLC

What a great story! There have been a number of times in my career and life where I wish I had known what this book has to teach!

DENNIS R. BRISCOE, Ph.D., Professor of International Human Resource Management, School of Business Administration, University of San Diego

Values-Based Leadership eloquently demonstrates that applying value-based leadership skills can single-handedly transform a failing company into a successful one. This engaging, story-like dialogue is a refreshing literary treat that brings home some simple, but incredibly valuable management techniques…read it!

ED STERNAGLE, Executive Director, University of California at Riverside Connect. Inducted to the Computer Hall of Fame, 1994

As a former basketball coach and an organizational leader, I felt an immediate connection with the lessons offered in this whimsical story on the importance of values in leadership. This story hits the bull's-eye!

JEFF BOWMAN, Fire Chief, City of San Diego, California

A delightful read! It's a modern day parable. I read it cover to cover absorbing wisdom, practical concepts and most importantly, tried and tested applications I can put to work today.

JAMES K. STEWART, Eagle Institute of Leadership, LLC

This important new book is the missing link in business books with its focus on the foundation of corporate life: how to build an ethical corporate culture. Majer delivers the real goods. It is a "must read" for the new millennium!

WILLIAM ALLEN, III, President, WELLTECH, Inc. and President, River Corporation

❧

This is a marvelous story with a great lesson about leadership. Every one of the 400 Chairs and all 8,000 CEO members of The Executive Committee should read it!

JOHN COTTER, Author of *Designing and Starting Up Greenfield Plants* and *20% Solution.* San Diego Chair, The Executive Committee

❧

Ken Majer's book on values is a timely parable for all who wish to live a life of balance and integrity at home and at work. It has great potential as a learning instrument, both in the adult training environment and in organizations. I shall be using it with students and clients as a purposeful and entertaining tool for developing leaders: for increasing their self-awareness and overall effectiveness in the workplace.

KAREN MILLER, Consultant/Trainer in Organizational Communication and visiting lecturer in Management Studies at the University of Cape Town, South Africa

❧

Values-Based Leadership *does an outstanding job demonstrating how personal and corporate values not only drive the behavior of individuals, but also drive how the company is reflected in the marketplace. This is a valuable tool for all people in positions of influence in today's business environment.*

RUSSELL AEBIG, Managing Partner, New Day Management Group

❧

*A revolution is about to begin in corporate America—
a movement to recover business ethics. Dr. Majer may
well lead this revolution with this practical book about
how to become a values-based leader. Read this book and
join the revolution!*

DR. TOM HILL, President, Eagle Institute, author of *Living at the
Summit* and co-author of *Chicken Soup for the Entrepreneurial Soul*

*A great story correlating Values with Strategic Direction.
That is the essence of business . . . .*

DAN WERTENBERG, Founder and CEO of Building Technologies

*All successful organizations need clearly stated values
that everyone knows and lives by every day. The message
in Ken Majer's story about how to develop and use
organizational values is universal. By following the
processes in this book, common sense will become
common practice.*

DAVID GLASSMAN, Visiting Fellow at the Cranfield School of
Management and London Chair, The Executive Committee

*For leaders seeking to build successful organizations and
companies comprised of energetic, passionate, and
committed employees, Values-Based Leadership provides
a roadmap for the journey. This provocative, engaging
story compels leaders to clarify their personal and
organizational values and offers valuable methods
through which we can accomplish this goal.*

SANFORD B. EHRLICH, PH.D., QUALCOMM Executive
Director of Entrepreneurship,
Entrepreneurial Management Center, San Diego State University

This book is small in size but mighty in its concepts! The vision of our corporations turning to values-based leadership as described in this delightful book gives me hope for the future.

ORIENNE STRODE, Founder and President,
Human Dimensions in Medical Education

This is a great work. I could not wait for the story to unfold! This book will be helpful to anyone who is looking for some direction to get back to the basics and isn't sure how to do that. I plan to use the concepts of values-based leadership immediately to resolve some of my client's concerns.

LARRY R. OHLHAUSER, MD, President and CEO,
Healthcare Solutions and Innovations, Inc.

Today's headlines describe our business environment as a planet with business leaders spinning in increasingly errant orbits, driven by misshapen and misplaced values. Ken Majer's timely and insightful work foretells the positive impact of values-based leadership and the strong gravitational force these principles can exert to pull individuals and companies back into a tighter, value-based trajectory.

JENIFER A. LANG, President and CEO,
Interface Displays & Controls, Inc.

Contents

Foreword

VALUES-BASED LEADERSHIP is a fast-paced, engrossing story of one CEO's dramatic awareness that his company is adrift, rudderless without a foundation of values to guide consistent behavior. The opening scene that shakes fear into the soul of Robb Reinhart is repeated all too often in real life by executives unaware they are on the precipice of impending disaster.

This engaging book reads like a fast-paced novel with twists and turns that dramatize practical yet profound principles and processes of leadership. The author's experiences and skills as a consultant and executive mentor are undoubtedly reflected in one of the book's main characters, "Coach," who becomes the alter ego to the story's lead protagonist.

Robb Reinhart literally receives his wake-up call

through a dream premonition of a board meeting that puts him on edge. But it is his wife's questioning that causes him to examine the underlying dynamics of a potential crisis. It is then he discovers that everyone in his company, including the chairman of the board, has sensed the signs of organizational disorder. Robb's preoccupation with performance metrics has blinded him to a variety of subtle clues that indicate his key people are diverging from *his* norms—*his* fundamental values—on which he thought the company was based.

Shaken to problem-solve in ways that depart from his usual business practices, Robb reengages his executive team by probing and reinterpreting employee survey data previously ignored. As he and his vice presidents drill down through the layers of management, a disturbing picture emerges: the organization is out of sync with the best practices it once enjoyed.

This story provides an artful interplay between an executive's philosophical point of view and his need to involve his team members in a progression of implementation actions. But the saga is not just focused on achieving improved business results. The events of the story also require the reader to consider the personal challenges of leaders as human beings with self-doubts and anxieties. One must also consider the teacher's role as mentor and confidant to team members, who at times may face deeply troubling personal or family crises. It keeps us mindful that, as leaders, we serve multiple audiences, any one of which may take center stage and demand attention.

Author Ken Majer is a compelling storyteller with a mission, but one who sustains the intrigue and flow of the story without rushing or forcing the leadership principles from which all of us can learn. Throughout, he guides the reader into critical thinking as Robb and Coach periodically engage in probing question-and-answer sessions.

The reader who reflects thoughtfully on this portfolio of lessons will be better prepared to respond to leadership challenges. Using the principles in *Values-Based Leadership* will go a long way toward helping meet these challenges in our increasingly complex and changing business world.

≈

CURTIS W. COOK
Dean and Professor of Management
School of Business Administration
University of San Diego

1

Fear at first—then wide awake.
Is this my life I have at stake?

⇝

"YOU'RE FIRED." The words hit Robb like an unexpected punch in the stomach. He felt faint, kind of giddy, and a little woozy—off balance.

The chairman's message was a shock. Robb Reinhart had been CEO of Central Plains Foods, a major Midwestern food distribution company, for three years after logging almost four years as the senior vice president of marketing followed by five years as the company's chief operating officer. While there had been some setbacks recently, this was completely unexpected. He was stunned.

Robb had come to the board of directors' meeting with the same confidence and nonchalance that he characteristically had: *No big deal. We'll talk the numbers, review the go-forward strategy, endure some of the self-importance of one or two of the directors, and adjourn the meeting. Then I'll go back to work at my real job—running the company.*

It was true that the company's business over the past two quarters was slower than usual, but the numbers weren't all that bad considering the economy, a world jittery with the reality of terrorism, and the aftermath of 9/11 still palpable. After all, people had to eat, and Central Plains Foods distributed produce to most of the major supermarket chains as well as the independent grocery stores in the eight-state Midwest region.

What should have alerted Robb to the impending doomsday message from Chairman Dr. Neil Anderson were the comments he made leading up to Robb's abrupt dismissal.

"My biggest concern is not the drop in revenues as you might suspect . . . it's the disintegration of our culture . . . the indifference of our employees . . . a malaise that is destroying the spirit of our team . . . and a callousness toward our suppliers. These are the failures of leadership that will doom any great company, and we must have a change at the top to avoid such a fate!"

Disintegrating culture, indifference, malaise, callousness. What in the world is he talking about?

As the chairman droned on with his accusations, Robb's vision tunneled and Anderson's body seemed to loom larger and larger at the end of the table. At the same time, his bellowing voice increased in intensity, filling the room and making it close and stuffy. He felt as though he were in a Kafka movie as Mary Meyers, vice president of

Human Resources, handed Robb the resignation papers to sign. The pen in his hand seemed heavy and slippery. The room felt hot, but Robb was chilled and damp.

≈

Stay in Touch

with Your Workforce.

2

When do we find "A Word to the Wise?"
Sometimes sleep will open our eyes.

"WAKE UP! WAKE UP, ROBB!" He heard his wife's voice from miles away. "Robb . . . Robb." He sat bolt upright in bed. In a cold sweat he realized that he had been dreaming.

"Sweetheart, are you feeling okay?" Sharon asked with concern. "You were moaning and groaning in your sleep and saying something about an 'unfair execution.' My goodness, you're all sweaty and shivering. Do you have a fever?"

"No, no. I'm okay. It was just a bad dream." Robb got up, fetched a glass of water, and put on a fresh pair of pyjamas. Before going back to bed, he stared into the bathroom mirror and thought he looked like he had been in a fight. He certainly felt that way.

What was that nightmare all about? I'm sure glad Sharon woke me up before it got worse. He stopped and remembered Sharon's voice urging him to wake up.

Maybe this was more than a dream. Maybe it really was a "wake-up" call.

The More Experience

You Have, the

Wiser It Is to

Listen to Your Gut!

3

Keeping my poise and acting normal,
searching for answers, however informal.

THAT MORNING AT BREAKFAST, Robb read the paper while he and Sharon shared coffee and muffins, their morning ritual.

"Don't forget Jimmy's soccer game tonight, Robb. It's my late night at work."

"Like I could forget, Sweetheart. You put a sticky note on the bathroom mirror, a picture of Jimmy in his soccer shirt in my briefcase, and your travel alarm clock set for 4:45 P.M. in my jacket pocket."

"Oh, did you notice?" Sharon asked in wide-eyed innocence.

"Very funny. Not to worry, I'll be there, and Jimmy and I will grab a bite to eat after the game. We'll be home around eight."

"Thanks, Babe. I know you have a busy schedule, but it means a lot to Jimmy when one of us is in the stands."

Sharon was truly a wonderful mom. In addition to her job as the marketing director for a local department store, she found time for volunteer work as a court-appointed special advocate for children from broken homes. She had many friends, but she still made it a point to place Jimmy at the top of her priority list. Both she and Robb helped him with homework, encouraged him with music, and went to his soccer games and swim meets whenever they could.

Sharon and Robb had agreed a long time ago that one of them would always be at Jimmy's sporting events. Usually they went together, but this particular evening was one of those occasions where Robb would attend the soccer game by himself.

"By the way," Sharon asked, "what was that dream you had last night? It really seemed to upset you."

"Oh, yeah. It was odd. I was in a board of directors' meeting and Neil Anderson was going off on a tangent complaining about a 'breakdown of the company culture,' and how our employees were 'callous and indifferent.' It was strange. Then it got really weird when Mary Meyers, my HR vice president—the person I hand-picked for the job four years ago—handed me my resignation papers and confirmed that I was fired!" Robb chuckled as he muttered, "Yeah, right, can you imagine . . . ." His voice trailed off as he pretended to reabsorb himself in the paper.

Sharon chuckled. "That'll be the day! You've been the sole leader, champion, and workhorse around there for over ten years." Her support was obvious. Stopping a moment and cocking her head over his newspaper, she masked her concern and asked, "What do you think it meant? Is something going on at work that you are conveniently forgetting to tell me?"

Robb straightened up and looked at her with a mocked stern expression. "Now don't get Freudian on me. Nothing is going on other than the impact of the economy and all the other pressures of the world that are stressing every business. We don't have any serious concerns. And the company employees, our business relationships—all is 'business as usual.' Maybe the electric blanket was turned up too high and the heat triggered the dream. Whatever. Not to worry."

He stood up, gave Sharon an affectionate kiss on the cheek, told her to have a great day, and said that he would look forward to seeing her around eight.

In his car on the way to work, however, he thought about what Sharon had asked him. *What was that about last night? Is there something going on that I don't know about? Are my employees truly callous and rude to customers, suppliers, and each other? The values that I have always espoused include fairness and courtesy. After all, that's how I treat others and my example should be clear to everyone in the organization. I have to check this out when*

I get to the office and dispel that silly little dream. One doesn't get "truth" in the middle of the night. He was unsettled.

The first thing Robb did when he got to the office, after the usual friendly greetings with his administrative assistant, Maria, was to call Mary Meyers. When she answered the phone, Robb asked, "Hey, Mary, am I still employed?"

"What?" she asked incredulously.

"Nothing, nothing, just a bad personal joke. Say, I'm calling because I would like to review the latest customer satisfaction survey. Would you mind bringing a copy when you have some time this morning and reviewing it with me for a few minutes? What time works for you? Great, I'll see you around 10:15. Thanks."

"Am I still employed?" Now where did that stupid comment come from?

Mary and Robb reviewed the survey results and Robb was more than a little concerned. "Mary, I didn't realize the scores were so low in some of these categories. Do we have other indications of dissatisfaction? What about our vendors, suppliers, and the unions?" Robb's voice tightened a bit and he began to fire rapid questions at Mary as was his habit when he felt pressure.

"Actually, I know we haven't spent a lot of time looking at these types of data, because it has never seemed to be a priority for you. But I have been concerned. So have Jack and Will—and some of the others on the executive committee. The low scores have been a trend over the last year." Jack Tymeson was Robb's chief operating officer and Will Brown was the company's vice president of marketing. Customer relations fell under Will's umbrella.

"Well, why haven't we been doing something about it?" Robb asked, a little too forcefully.

"Easy, Robb, don't shoot the messenger," Mary cautioned, staring back at Robb and keeping her ground. "You haven't exactly been open to looking at these matters for some time. It's always seemed that your faith in our market leadership, revenue, and profitability indicators were the most important objectives. And you may be right."

"I'm sorry, Mary. No, *you're* right. I have not paid much attention to satisfaction data. I've been focused on bottom line performance. That's my job. But if you and the rest of the executive team think we should be paying more attention to other key indicators, then maybe I have been a little remiss. Let's take a walk."

Follow Your

Hunches, but

Check Out

the Facts!

4

You see things anew—you don't like it much.
It seems that you've lost your Midas touch.

❦

ROBB ACCOMPANIED MARY down the hall to Jack's office. The COO wasn't in. His administrative assistant seemed nervous amid their presence and said a little too hastily, "I'm not exactly sure where he is this morning, Mr. Reinhart. He's usually here bright and early. Would you like him to come and see you when he arrives?"

"That's okay. Just have him give me a call when he gets in, Heather." Robb glanced at Mary to get a sense from her if she thought anything was unusual about Jack not being in and not letting his assistant know his whereabouts, but Mary gave no clues.

"Let's go see if Will's around," he suggested and led Mary off toward his marketing guru's office.

Will was in, on the phone, and talking animatedly in a fairly loud voice. His door was open and Robb could hear Will chiding someone on the other end of the line. "I don't care what happened, Tom. Your report indicates that you will miss your numbers for the second month in a row. Not a good sign. You have one more month before the end of the quarter, and I expect you to get your act together by then. See you later." And he hung up.

"Hi Mary, Robb. What brings you slumming this morning?" he said good-naturedly. "Did you come down just to see how to light a fire under one of our sales reps who's not cutting the mustard?"

"No, not really, Will. But it's good to see that at least you're here at your desk this morning."

"Of course, I'm here. I work here, remember?" Will continued with his lighthearted banter.

"Just kidding. What I really want to do is chat with you about the customer satisfaction survey that Mary completed recently. I realize that I haven't always paid close attention to some of the 'softer' performance indica-tors like employee and customer satisfaction, but Mary is helping me to see that these may provide some important clues about the slowdown that we've seen in the past couple of months."

Will feigned surprise. "Really? Robb, the original hard numbers man, is going to look at the soft side?" Then he got serious. "Actually, I agree with Mary. We need to exam-ine some of the reasons behind our slowing business performance. It's not just the economy. In fact, recent trends are showing strong improvement in our industry as well as many others. A number of us have been trying to think of how to approach you on the subject."

"Well, here I am, Will. Approach away," Robb said as he slid into a chair across from Will's desk. Mary sat in another chair next to Robb.

"Well, you've asked, so I do have a couple of ideas. The survey seems to indicate that some of our customers are unhappy with us. I'm not sure why, but my hunch is that our people are overpromising to get sales, which is forcing others in the company to work extra hard to deliver. In other cases, our people seem to be a little complacent because we've been acknowledged as the leader in the Midwest. I'm not sure what's behind it. Perhaps we should conduct a more in-depth study and dig a little deeper. What do you think, Mary?"

"I think it's a solid idea to probe a little more. But it doesn't have to be a big research effort. Each of us on the executive team could bring our managers together and have a discussion about the survey results. They're closer to the customers and they could have some insights."

"Good idea," Robb added, "but let's put a little structure around the discussion. Perhaps we could ask them to brainstorm the answers to a few questions. For instance, do you think the recent customer satisfaction survey results are an accurate reflection of how our customers view Central Plains Foods? What do you think is the cause of the negative survey results? And how much do you think the views of our customers are affecting our sales and profitability?"

Will and Mary seconded Robb's thinking and were pleased that he was taking an interest in this side of the business. All three of them agreed that the seven members of the executive team should bring their managers together, conduct the brainstorm session, and send a brief summary to Mary who would integrate the results for Robb. Eager to move on this, Robb said he would put out a memo to the team: Mary and Will plus Jack, the COO; Danielle Doyle, the CFO; Mark Peavey, VP of warehouse and distribution; Alicia Ramirez, VP of purchasing and administration; and Wanda Fong, the CIO.

Robb wrote the memo and emailed it to his team, attended his son's soccer game that evening, and went about his normal routine—until a week later, that is.

Mary's report was on his desk Thursday morning. It was enough to make Robb sit up and take notice. As he read through the report, he could feel his blood pressure rising. First of all, Mary appended a note that Jack did not conduct his session, so his data weren't included. Jack gave the excuse that his people were too busy. If that wasn't disturbing enough, the opinions of the managers made it worse. As he read through the report, a few of the comments stood out.

Do you think the recent customer satisfaction survey results are an accurate reflection of how our customers view Central Plains Foods?

✔ Yes, and if we are not careful, it will get worse instead of better.

✔ I'm not sure it really matters if they are super-happy or not. They need what we have, and we are the leader in the region.

✔ Are we supposed to be trying to make our customers happy or delivering food?

⇌

What do you think is the cause of the negative survey results?

✔ We don't know what to tell our customers because we don't know what's going on in our own company. We are confused, so the customers are confused and don't know what to expect.

✔ We don't spend any time training our front-line people on how to act with customers.

✔ We don't have a policy on how to deal with customer complaints. It's done on an ad hoc basis.

✔ If we spent more time delivering food to our customers instead of spending all this time taking surveys and sitting around flapping our gums about it, the customers would not be complaining. This is a waste of time and a pain in the butt!

How much do you think the views of our customers are affecting our sales and profitability?

✔ Not at all.

✔ Totally. I fear we are going to go out of business if we don't pay more attention to our customers.

~

The only consolation Robb could take from these comments was that at least they seemed honest. *But what was this about? This doesn't sound like the company I've led for over a decade. I thought everyone at Central Plains felt the same way I do about people, and realized the importance of gathering data for continuous improvement. Who are these people? I thought we were all in sync, but it sure doesn't seem that way!*

Just then, Maria walked in and interrupted his thoughts. "You okay, Boss?" she asked. "You look a little stressed." She handed him some paperwork and his messages.

"Yeah, fine, Maria. But I'm a little surprised at what I'm finding in this report from Mary."

"Oh, the one about the manager brainstorm sessions? Everyone's talking about them."

Robb looked up. "What do you mean, 'everyone's talking about them?'"

"Nothing, really. It just seems as though the customer survey and the follow-up brainstorm conversations have hit the gossip wires."

"Oh, great!" Robb moaned. "That's just what I need."

"Well, maybe this message will help. Dr. Anderson would like you to call him first thing tomorrow morning. He wants to schedule an interim board of directors' meeting."

Gather Insights from Everyone.

And Remember:

The Only Thing

More Important than

Asking Questions

Is Listening to the Answer!

5

Confused and afraid, distracted at best,
an answer appears—or is this a test?

~≥~

ROBB LEFT THE OFFICE at a quarter to five and drove
to the soccer field. He was down in the dumps. It wasn't
his nature to feel like this. *Why a special board meeting
now?* Robb had a tough time concentrating on his son's
participation in the game. He was lost in thought.

"Say, isn't that your son wearing number three?" asked
a distant voice.

"Yep, that's my boy Jimmy." Robb responded without
looking to his right where the old man's deep voice was
coming from.

"Well, that was a great save he just made, Dad."

Robb turned slowly and looked at the gentlemen sitting next to him. He had been unaware that anyone was
there. The older gent had a thick white beard and was
wearing a warm-up jacket with a large V on the left side
of the chest that Robb noted was the athletic symbol for

the local university, Vicksburg State. He also wore a ball cap with "Coach" stitched on the visor. Beneath the visor Robb could see a set of bushy eyebrows and startling blue eyes. He had never understood the concept of "twinkling eyes" until this moment.

"Hi, I'm Bobby Olson. But no one ever remembers my name. They just call me Coach." He extended his strong, warm hand and Robb responded with, "Hello, Coach. I'm . . . ."

"Robb Reinhart, Jimmy's dad. Yeah, I know. I've been watching all the kids in this league and how the parents encourage the kids. Between you and your wife, you never miss a game. I'd say that's one of the reasons Jimmy is tearing up the turf. He feels your support."

"Well, thanks, Coach. We're very proud of Jimmy and want to support him as much as we can."

"That's one of the reasons I like coming out to watch the young kids, to see if my theory is still valid." He stopped and let his comment hang in the air, anticipating correctly that Robb would not let the "theory" reference go by.

Robb took the bait. "What theory is that, Coach?"

"You see, Mr. Reinhart, when I was coaching at the college level, I took notice of what made teams and individuals great on the field. Once I understood the secret, winning became a piece of cake. We won four division championships and had two national rankings in my final six years at Vicksburg State. *It was all about having the right values.* Teams that had them won. Teams that didn't have 'em, didn't win. The fun part for me now is to watch the same thing going on with these kids."

"Just what do you mean by 'the right values,' Coach? I thought there was just one value in sports: *Play hard to win.*" Robb's interest in what the older man had to say was piqued.

"Getting kids to play hard doesn't necessarily produce champions. There are a few more ingredients. Talent, of course, is essential—and many kids have terrific talent—but the wrong attitude. The right attitude is essential for winning. *But you know all that,* Mr. Reinhart. The real question is: Where does the winning attitude come from?"

"Brilliant coaches?" Robb offered.

"Good try. Flattery will usually get you somewhere, but not this time. Coaches can only recognize and nurture winning attitudes. The attitudes themselves come from within the kids. It's about what they believe in their hearts. It's about knowing what's important—about what's important to them. And these winning beliefs and attitudes come from the personal *values* the kids hold."

"Take a look at any team, maybe even your top executive team at Central Plains Foods. If the team is performing well, my bet is that it's because the members have a common sense of what's important. That common sense of what's important is what drives the team. Don't you see it that way, Mr. Rienhart?"

Robb wanted to ask Bobby Olson how he knew that he worked at Central Plains and that he had the top team reporting to him. In fact, he suddenly had a whole bunch of questions he wanted to ask Coach. But Robb was distracted by the final whistle, the elated fans, and the players celebrating another victory. Jimmy's team won again, 3-1. He spotted Jimmy and gave him a congratulatory "thumbs up" and looked over to continue his chat with Mr. Olson, only to see the old gent turn toward Robb and give him a two-finger V-for-Victory wave as he stepped off of the stands. The twinkle in his eye beyond his Santa Claus beard was clear from thirty feet away.

&

Your Values

Drive Your Behavior.

6

*The values are there, right on the wall,
but if we don't live by them, they're no help at all!*

THE NEXT MORNING, after Robb kissed Sharon good-bye, he noticed that he had a vague sense of dread. He had not slept well. He was preoccupied with his conversation with Coach. He wondered just who this Bobby Olson was. Apparently, he was real because Robb searched for him on the Internet and found the victory record from fifteen years back at Vicksburg State. Olson's name was there—as the coach.

Robb asked Sharon and Jimmy if either of them knew anything about the old man called Coach. Sharon said she's overheard some of the other soccer moms making favorable comments about the man named "Coach," and then Jimmy confirmed that Coach was almost always at the soccer games and frequently watched the practices. He never bothered anyone and everyone seemed to know and like him. Jimmy described him as sort of a "wise old

Gramps who really knows the game." He told Robb that his soccer coach often asked the older man's advice.

What was Coach trying to tell me about the kids who knew inside what was important? Were these the athletes who had an inner sense of what drove them to extraordinary levels of success on the playing field? What did he mean about having the right beliefs and attitudes coming from their personal values?

The first thing Robb did when he got to the office was to look up the word "values." The best definitions he could come up with that matched what Coach was talking about were "esteemed qualities," "intrinsically desirable," or "having importance." The dictionary didn't help much.

Coach was talking about something different. He was saying that what people value and hold dear is important— that strongly held values shape their beliefs and attitudes. And their beliefs and attitudes, in turn, determine how they act. Coach's teams must have valued winning, success, strength, talent, excellence, and other attributes of winners.

Robb looked at the framed document above his credenza. It contained a nicely designed parchment entitled "Our Values at Central Plains." Without reading down to the list of values written in an Old English Text font that had been selected to give the values a sense of history and stability, he closed his eyes to see if he could remember the five words that were supposed to be the guiding principles of Central Plains' business. He couldn't remember the last time he had glanced at the list, much less thought about how these values influenced his decision-making or management style.

It took a minute for Robb to remember all five of the words. In fact, had he not remembered HIPPO, the acronym he came up with to help others memorize them, he may not have been able to recall them at all. Robb smiled to himself sheepishly as he remembered telling his staff, who thought it a little corny but fun, "Remember HIPPO because these are *big* ideas!"

Honesty
Integrity
Profits
People
Opportunity

Where did these company values come from? Well, they came from me, didn't they? Or, in Coach's words, they came from within me. He's right. These are the values I grew up with. I can remember Dad using one of his pet expressions whenever I had a question of right or wrong: "Honesty is the best policy." And his other rule to live by: "You are only as good as your word. That's what it means to have integrity."

Later, when growing up and wondering what career to choose, I remember talking with Grandpa under the huge hickory tree in the backyard of his summer cottage and his counseling me in his heavy European accent, "You must have a profitable business."

And, Mom, bless her heart, she's the one who instilled the idea that helped me gain popularity in high school and success throughout college and my career: "Always think of other people first, and you will never want for anything."

Opportunity. That one came from Mr. Kent, my high school biology teacher. "In science as in life," he repeated many times throughout that sophomore year, "there is boundless opportunity."

Amazing! Coach was right. The values that have guided my life were instilled in me a long time ago. No wonder I chose those values as the foundation for running the company.

But something was wrong. And Robb knew it. He thought about Will "lighting a fire" under one of his sales reps. Was Will thinking about other people first, or was he thinking about his division's performance? Jack had neglected to bring his managers together to discuss the survey results as he had agreed. He said he would, but he didn't. Where was the integrity in that? And, many of the reactions to the survey discussions certainly did not reflect the intention of the values we have for the company.

Something wasn't working. People were not living the values of the company. They were not behaving on the job the way the values suggested they should.

Robb asked Maria to come into his office. "Maria, I'd like you to do a little quiet surveillance for me," he requested.

"Hmmm, this sounds intriguing," she replied, rubbing her hands together and raising her eyebrows.

"I'd like you to conduct a little informal survey of the senior staff's office areas and the general administrative offices. Just take a look around when you are going about your regular business and count the number of times you find a copy of these company values hanging on the wall." He pointed to the framed document in his office.

Later that afternoon, Maria reported back. Robb was truly surprised. In addition to copies in the lobby, the lunchroom, the copy room, and in public areas through-out the building, most of the executives and managers had them in their offices. Maria counted twenty-seven copies in all. Robb was initially pleased that the company had saturated the office environment with these guiding principles until Maria laughed and said she must have walked past them hundreds of times and never even noticed they were there!

The problem was obvious. The employees didn't even *see* the values, much less live by them. The popular adage was true: we at Central Plains were "talking the talk" but we aren't "walking the walk." But why?

Stating Your Values

Is Nothing.

Living Your Values

Is Everything!

7

The teacher comes back, as if right on cue,
just when the student opens in you.

~

ROBB WAS PACING in his office. It was around 11:00 A.M.
and he had just talked with the chairman about setting up
the special board meeting in two weeks. He couldn't get
much out of Dr. Anderson about the agenda. *Is Anderson
being mysterious or am I getting paranoid?*

Robb dialed Sharon's number to talk with her about
how he was feeling, but he hung up before the call went
through. He didn't want to upset her needlessly over what
could be absolutely nothing.

What he really wanted to do was to talk with Coach
again to gain some additional insight about the importance
of values and how they contributed to a winning team. He
was still unnerved by Coach's uncanny knowledge about
his executive team, and by knowing who Robb was. It
wasn't exactly creepy, but certainly intriguing.

There was no soccer game that week. The league had

the week off. Robb was sure Coach would have been there if a game had been scheduled, but he didn't think he would find him in an empty set of bleachers.

Maria tried to find a Bobby Olson in the phone directory. No listing. The operator had said there was a Robert Olson, but the number was unlisted. His usual sources were drying up. He was just about to call Jimmy's soccer coach and ask if he knew how to get in touch with the old man when Maria stuck her head through the doorway.

"You're not going to believe this, Boss, but there's a Mr. Bobby Olson on the line for you . . . . "

For an instant, the hair on the back of Robb's neck stood up, but the feeling was quickly replaced with relief. He picked up the phone.

"Coach?"

"Hello, Mr. Reinhart, I hope I'm not interrupting you."

"Quite the contrary, I've been thinking about you this morning, and even tried to find your phone number. I wanted to talk with you about some of the things you said to me last Thursday night just before the game ended."

As Coach chuckled, Robb had an image of the light behind those piercing blue eyes. Coach continued, "I thought about that this morning, too. I'm sorry I had to run off so quickly the other night, but I had an important obligation. I've been thinking ever since that maybe you would like to continue our conversation about values."

"You bet. That's why I was trying to reach you. When I realized there was no game tonight, getting together became even more important. It has to do with some things that are going on here at Central Plains. To be honest, I thought I could use a little coaching from you. Are you free for lunch?"

"Sure am, and a bit hungry, too."

"Name the place, Coach, and I'll meet you at noon. The University Club at the top of the Symphony Building or the Sporting Lounge at the Fairmont Hotel, you name it."

"Actually, Mr. Reinhart," Coach hesitated, "if you don't mind, how about Henry's Hot Dogs, the stand in the park? Hank serves a mean Polish sausage with sauerkraut."

"You got it!" Robb laughed. "And, by the way, it's 'Robb.' I haven't been called 'Mr. Reinhart' since I was a freshman in ROTC."

"Okay, Robb. See you in the park at noon."

Coach greeted Robb with the same V-for-Victory wave as he walked up to Henry's. They ordered, then sat together on a bench wiping the mustard and sauerkraut juice from their fingers and sipping on a couple of soft drinks when Robb launched into the problem he was having at Central Plains.

Robb described what he now termed the "values crisis." He related his disappointment with Jack and Will and went so far as to disclose the dream he had, the harbinger of this whole values fiasco. He shared his discomfort about

the upcoming special board meeting and ended by admitting that he was a little embarrassed about dumping his
problem on Coach, his new friend. "You're certainly easy
to talk to, and a great listener," he added.

Coach had not taken his eyes off Robb except to pitch
his crumpled napkin and sandwich wrap into a wire trash
basket twelve feet away. A perfect "swish."

After what seemed to be a long silence, Coach asked,
"Okay if I throw a few questions at you?"

"Sure."

"You have a set of corporate values, don't you?"

"Yes, I do. I've thought about it quite a bit. Like you
suggested about the great athletes, those values came from
within me. The company values are framed in my office:

Honesty, Integrity, Profits,
People and Opportunity.

And I think I live by them. At least I try to."

"I believe you do," Coach replied. "It's clear to me by
the way you interact with Jimmy. *People*—Jimmy comes
first in your life. *Integrity*—you say you are coming to the
games on Thursday, and you do . . . almost always on
time," he grinned. "And what's more, I can see the values
transferring to Jimmy. He looks for *opportunity* on the
field. When he screws up, he *honestly* admits it. I'd bet
you even use some of the same phrases with Jimmy that
you heard in your youth, such as 'He's as honest as the

day is long.'"

"I never realized it, but yeah, I guess I do use some of those same phrases that I heard growing up. Must be genetic," Robb mused.

Coach continued his questions. "Where do those values reside?"

"In twenty-seven places all over the office."

"Where else?"

Robb thought. "In me."

"Precisely."

"Whose values are they?"

"Mine."

"You're a quick study. Now, who do you want to live by these values?" Coach pressed on.

"Everyone in the company."

"Why?"

"Because I believe those values provide a great code of ethics for us to maintain a winning company," Robb said with conviction.

"Again, whose values are they?"

"Mine."

"And where do they come from?"

"Within me."

"Now, tell me," Coach asked, "if people act on what *they* believe to be important, what drives their behavior?"

"Their values."

"Whose values?"

"*Their* values."

"*Their own* values," Coach added. "And whose values are on the wall in twenty-seven places at Central Plains?"

"Mine," Robb turned to look directly at Coach. "Oh," and then, "Duh!" as he slapped his forehead in mock enlightenment. "The folks at work are not living the values, *because the values did not come from them.*"

Coach looked at Robb, raised his bushy grey eyebrows, and waited.

"But Coach," Robb put on his best air of executive reasoning, "I am the chief executive officer. Their leader. I'm expected to set the stage, show the way, and all that."

"Yep, you are expected to 'walk the walk' indeed. You must lead—or you will have no followers. But don't ever forget that true leadership is when your followers *want* to follow you, not because they are *coerced* to follow you. And what better way to align a team of people than to uncover the values that are most important to them as well as to you?"

Coach let that sink in.

The Sign of a

Great Leader Is

When People

Want to Follow.

8

Now you know how to build a great team,
but aligning everyone is a challenging theme.

≈

COACH WAITED UNTIL he could see that Robb grasped the importance of having his team create their own set of values to live and work by, then added, "Let me tell you about my championship teams at Vicksburg State." He pointed to the large V on his warm-up jacket and went on to share with Robb how he discovered and nurtured the values within his talented young players to create what he called a "winning culture" for his teams.

He explained that after every practice and every game, he would "debrief" with his players. They would discuss what they thought went well that day and what could be improved. Coach always started with what he called the "delta"—the Greek symbol representing change—and asked the question, "What could we have done better today?"

After discussing ways to improve, the team was asked what they did particularly well that day. This served a number of purposes, not the least of which was to get everyone feeling good about the team before going home. In addition, Coach would then "peel the onion" to get to a deeper level of understanding. He would ask why a particular play or drill was successful. The players would offer reasons such as, "I knew I could count on Kenny to be in the right spot for that pass because we had practiced it so many times and we had talked about what a great fake it would be."

Coach would ask, "What did you know about Kenny that gave you the confidence to make that pass?"

"I *trusted* him. I know that he wants to do his best to help the team. We've talked about making this into a winning team many, many times."

At this point in these debriefs, Coach would engage the rest of the team to express their thoughts about when things just "clicked" in practice or a game. After many seasons of these debriefing sessions during which the players uncovered what was important to them about creating winning teams, Coach said he discovered the same values appearing over and over again: trust, commitment, accountability, teamwork, communication, and fair play.

"By the time I found this secret to developing winning teams," Coach explained to Robb, "I became wise enough never to introduce those values that I was pretty confident they would come up with by themselves. I had to let the concepts come from within them. That is what made it valuable. These words that guided them to play their hearts out represented what was truly important to each of them. They became the team's values, not my values. It just so happened, I was in perfect agreement with the values that they came up with!"

"Coach, I think I've got it. I'm not sure how to do it at Central Plains, but I can see that I've got to involve my team in creating the company's values if I ever hope to get everyone on board and pulling in the same direction. Do you have any ideas for me?"

"Oh, maybe one or two," Coach smiled his answer. "Here's an approach you might try at your next executive team meeting . . . ."

❧

The Secret to Building a

Winning Team Is

Helping Team Members

Discover Their Own

Set of Values and

Helping Them to

Act on Them.

❧

9

Setting the stage and preparing for change,
the environment must be adroitly arranged.

❧

ROBB WAS READY. At least he thought he was. Introducing his unhappiness with how employees in the company were acting was going to be tricky. But he was determined to get to the bottom of what was going on and see if the poor employee satisfaction had anything to do with the beliefs and attitudes among his top executives.

He called a two-hour meeting of his executive team at 10:00 A.M. on Wednesday morning. Everyone was there: Jack, Danielle, Mary, Alicia, Mark, Wanda, and Will. Robb also added Brett Mayberg, the company's outside legal counsel.

Brett was more than their lawyer. He and Robb had been close friends in college and best man in each other's weddings. Robb had relied on Brett as his business lawyer and confidant throughout his career. Brett knew as much about Robb and how he operated as anyone.

Only Jack, Danielle, and Brett formally reported directly to Robb. As COO, Jack supervised Alicia, Wanda, Mark, Will, and Mary, but Robb had an open door policy, and everyone felt comfortable discussing issues directly with him. However, he was always careful to have directives to Jack's managers come through Jack.

Robb mused about what an extraordinary group of people he had been able to put together as everyone got their coffee. *They are diverse, independent thinkers. Each one is exceptionally talented . . . but are they a cohesive team? Are they all team players? Sure, they had their disagreements, but wasn't that a sign of a healthy team?*

"Hi, everyone. Thanks for getting together on such short notice. I really appreciate the effort," Robb welcomed them. "As some of you know, Dr. Anderson is calling a special board meeting in a couple of weeks and I want to be sure that we're on top of our game. So, I need to be briefed fully on any issues that may be important. I've not yet seen the agenda for the meeting, but I'd really like to be prepared for anything that might come up."

"So what's new?" Will chided playfully. Appreciative smiles appeared around the room.

"In addition," Robb went on, "I want to be sure we've had a chance to discuss the employee survey summary that Mary prepared for us based on the discussions you had with your managers. I think the board may be interested in what we are doing about the results." That comment quieted people down, and Jack looked a little uncomfortable, yet Robb continued and was able to keep his momentum from faltering.

"First, I'd like to try something a little new this morning." He stopped and waited for everyone's full attention. "We spend a lot of hours here at Central Plains and most of the time we're all very busy and focused on our jobs. This is a pretty big operation. I know we have the company picnic in July and the annual holiday party, and some of us actually socialize together a bit. But lately, I've been thinking that we may not know each other as well as we think we do. So let me ask each of you the same question as we get started this morning: *How do you like to spend your time when you're not working?*"

A silence hovered over the room as everyone gazed at each other in amazement at this odd question from the company president.

Uncover the Values

of a Team by

Asking the Members this

Simple Question:

How do You

Spend Your Time

When You're Not Working?

10

*Touching the feelings inside of each heart
brings teams together, never apart.*

⌇

AS USUAL, Will piped up and broke the ice. "Well, boss, as you know, I'm always working! I never stop. I rarely sleep or eat, unless it's food from Central Plains, of course, and the company is my constant concern." A few groans, rolling eyes, and comments such as, "Sucking up, again, Will?" and "Gimme a break!" followed.

"Okay, I'm serious about this," Robb continued. "Most of us have been together for a lot of years. Wanda, you have the shortest tenure, a little over a year. I'll bet there are some interesting things for us to learn about you. So let's start with you. What do you like to do when you're not working?"

Wanda was known to be a technology wizard and a remarkable manager. Not only did she know just about everything there was to know about information and technology, she could inspire IT professionals to produce tremendous results without overworking them. She made the people on her team feel valuable and smart. People assumed she probably spent all of her spare time on the Internet or buried in the latest IT literature.

"Well . . . ," she began, a little tentatively, but clearly pleased about what she was about to reveal, "ever since I was a little girl, I've wanted to be a singer. So I sing every chance I get. I sing in my church choir, I sing at a Cantonese supper club in Chinatown and, believe it or not, I sing karaoke around town whenever I can. And, yes, I even sing in the shower!"

"You're kidding!" It was Danielle. "I studied voice at Indiana University. Actually, I selected IU because of the incredible music school they have. But after two years, I switched to finance at my parent's urging to have a career to fall back on and I just never got into singing professionally."

Then Mark Peavey spoke up. Mark was a bit of a rough-and-tumble guy and the most unlikely candidate, at least on the surface, to have an interest in music. "That's really interesting, Wanda. My son, Mark Jr., wants to be a singer. After figuring out that he couldn't hit the broad side of a barn with a football, my wife convinced me that we should let him follow his own dream."

"That's great!" Wanda said.

"He's applied for a special program at Juilliard. His audition is this week. He and my wife are in New York right now and I'm sitting on pins and needles waiting to hear if he made the cut. I'd really love for you to share your experiences with him. We don't know very many adult role models for him in music."

It was amazing to watch. After listening to this discussion, Robb continued to ask the question about what people did when they weren't working. Almost every time someone disclosed what was really important to him or her, someone else in the room connected in one way or another. Brett shared his interest in horses, and Alicia told him about her uncle's thoroughbred farm. Alicia relaxed with gardening and Will had a small greenhouse and grew rare orchids.

Mary trained for marathons and Robb admitted his dream was to be a triathlete. Jack was an investment fanatic and did some of his own trading. Wanda knew of some new software programs for asset management that might interest Jack. On it went for about forty minutes. The time flew by.

Then Robb decided it was time to take it to the next level.

Discovery Is Personal . . .

And It Can be Fun!

11

*Success, trust, balance—and even some fun—
define who we are and what makes us run.*

～

ROBB FELT GOOD about the way his team was becoming
more aware of each other and what made each of them tick.
Now he wanted to dig a little deeper.

"Jack," he probed, "what do you like about making
your own investment decisions?"

"Well, let's see . . . I think I like the sense of accom-
plishment when I've made a good investment," he said,
"and I don't like other people handling my financial
affairs—especially when they make poor decisions and I
lose money."

Robb scanned the group. "What do you think is behind
this? What is driving Jack? What's really important to him?
Let's see if we can put our finger on it."

"Show me the MONEY!" Will blurted out in his best
Cuba Gooding, Jr. imitation. Jack laughed appreciatively
but said that while money was important, that really was

not the most important driver.

"Then what is, Mary? What do you think is important to Jack about trading stocks?" Robb continued to probe.

"I think Jack wants to be in control of his own destiny." She replied. "We've all observed Jack at work. He watches things pretty carefully. He plans, holds everyone's feet to the fire, and keeps a high performance standard for himself. Same with his investing. Call him 'Mr. Accountability.'"

"So one of the *values* that motivates Jack's behavior is *accountability*," Robb stated rather than asked. Mary agreed, and Jack confirmed that he thought that was probably true.

"Alicia, spending time in your garden is clearly very important to you. What is it that gardening does for you?"

Alicia took a breath and relaxed, leaning back in her chair. "When I'm outside in my garden on a warm, sunny day, I get completely lost in my thoughts and the beauty of the plants and flowers. It's the most relaxing time I ever have. I love getting my hands in the dirt, tending the flower beds so the plants can flourish, then standing back and seeing the results weeks later. It's almost like being a mother again. And it's certainly a respite from paperwork, purchase orders, accounts receivable, and the stress of this place!" She mocked disdain for her work environment and the administrative tasks that everyone knew she loved and handled so well.

"Brett, you've known Alicia a long time. In fact, your families get together. What do you think is behind Alicia's passion for gardening? What is important to her about it?" Robb continued to push to the level of the values behind the actions.

"A couple of things, Robb. Alicia, correct me if I'm wrong, but I think you value the serenity of gardening because it's in contrast to your hectic work schedule. You love both, but it's the *balance* and the calming nature of gardening that gives you the energy you need to be the administrative whiz you are.

"In addition, you're a wonderful mother. You've done a great job raising your kids, and I've seen you use some of those skills around here as well as in your home. You are a very *nurturing* person, and God love ya for it!"

Suiting her character, but uncharacteristically spontaneous, Alicia got up, walked over to Brett's chair, gave him a hug, and said, "Thanks, Brett. That means a lot to me." Everyone applauded.

Robb had written *accountability* on the white board. He added *balance* and *nurturing* to the list. Continuing in this vein, Robb led the discussion until all the members on the team had shared why their outside interests were important. Each time someone explained his or her reasons, Robb asked the rest of the team to deduce the values that were behind the reasons. In less than an hour, he had written thirty-two values on the board. He pointed to the list.

"This is one heck of a list of values!" he said as he read them aloud.

Accountability

Life Balance

Nurturing

Independence

Achievement

Learning

Business Success

Fairness

Respect

Integrity

Honesty

Excellence

Precision

Reliability

Flexibility

Simplicity

Personal Success

Kindness

Humor

Fun

Strong Family Unit

Teamwork

Hard work

Communication

Commitment

Trust

Customer Satisfaction

Dependability

Having Vision

Creativity

Confidence

Being Focused

"How are we doing? Are you finding this exercise useful?" Robb asked.

"Absolutely—it's very enlightening," was the unanimous reply.

"All right. Let's take a short break. Come back in ten minutes and I'll share with you where we're going with this. I promised we'd be finished by noon. That will give us about another half-hour."

≈

*

When You Examine

What You Love to

Do Most,

Your Real Character

Will Emerge.

*

12

State confidently the goals you seek.
Being a leader is not for the meek.

⁓

EVERYONE WAS BACK in five minutes. They were obviously eager to continue. After all, they were talking about what was most important to them.

"Okay, everyone. Here's my two-minute soapbox speech for the day. I have learned recently—yes, old dog, new tricks—*that you are the same person everywhere you go.* You are no different at work than you are at home or at play, unless you're schizophrenic.

"Moreover, you are what you do. Aristotle said it best: *We are what we repeatedly do. Excellence then is not an act but a habit.*

"In other words, the way you behave reflects your attitude toward life. And your attitudes are a function of what you believe. These attitudes and beliefs are driven by what is most important to you—*your values.*"

Robb went to the white board and drew three boxes

next to the list of values:

He explained the diagram forward and backward emphasizing the arrows depicting two directions. "What you do is a function of your attitudes, which are a function of your beliefs, which are based on what is important to you—*your values.*

"Now here's the most important part for me. *You* are the leadership in this company. *Your* values reflect the values of Central Plains Foods. They are the same values that you hold dear at home and at play. You are the same person here that you are anywhere else. And together we set the tone and establish the culture for the entire company—based on our values."

Robb paused. He wondered who on the team would be the first to see where he was going with this.

"And our values," he continued, "define everything about the way we do business: how we hire, how we reward our employees, our relationships with our customers, our business processes, our systems, our procedures, our service philosophy, how we interact with each other—*everything.*"

Robb waited a moment while he observed a couple of fidgets and some reflective looks on a few faces. Then he said, "You will recall we've already established a set of values for the company." He pointed to one of the twenty-seven copies of the Central Plains' values that was hanging on the conference room wall: honesty, integrity, profit, people, opportunity.

"Time for a little self-disclosure," he continued. "Does anyone remember how these values came about?"

Jack and Brett both said that they remembered that the values were introduced at the first executive meeting they had offsite after Robb was promoted to CEO. Mary added that they sort of mysteriously appeared. Alicia could recall only that Robb's assistant, Maria, had asked her about where to take them to get framed.

"Right." Robb disclosed further. "I wrote those values. They were mine. They weren't created by all of us as a team. I won't ask you to share your answers to these questions, but let's put them on the table: How many of you have memorized these five values? How often have you referred to them with other employees?

"My guess is, most of you would answer 'no' and 'never.' Don't get me wrong! I'm not being critical. In fact, *even I've never referred to them since the day they were introduced.* So, why should you promote a set of values when you had nothing to do with creating them? I was foolish enough to expect you to endorse them just because they're mine.

"And it has not escaped my attention that two of the values from the list I created don't even appear on the list you generated today. Of course, three of my original five are included, and for that I'm grateful. So, if you don't mind, I would like to add *opportunity* and *people* to your list."

He went to the list and added his two values. "Oh, by the way," he said, "I am very happy with the rest of the list. With my two additions, I'm with you 100 percent!

"Now, here's our challenge. We can't have a list of thirty-four core values for our company. It would be too confusing and no one would be able to remember them, much less use them as guides for their actions. One of our values is *simplicity*, so let's exercise that principle.

"It's not going to be easy to cull this fine list to just four to six core values. I remember the story about a person who commented at the end of a letter to a friend, 'I'm sorry this letter is so long. I didn't have time to write a shorter one.' Simple is smart, but it isn't easy."

Robb then explained a process that would help them decide which values from the list would become the core values for the company. They would use a simple voting process. He explained that each of them would have three votes. Robb directed them to select the values they believed were most important by putting a check mark next to each one. Each team member could use one vote on three different values, two votes on one value and one on another, or all three votes on one value if they felt that strongly about it.

Robb encouraged everyone to go up to the white

board and discuss the merits of the values, decide, and vote. Some tension arose, a few jokes were cracked, but mainly each team member reviewed the list thoughtfully and placed his or her check marks next to the words that Robb had written on the white board.

In the end, it was clear. Robb circled the five values that had the most votes and nodded approvingly. "Well, how do you feel about our new set of core values?"

Customer Satisfaction

Trust

Communication

Learning

Respect

There were thoughtful, approving nods all around. "They're good." "I like them." "Solid." "Pretty exciting." Then someone noticed that they had just worked through the noon hour.

"I'm sorry about going over the time limit," Robb said sincerely.

"I guess we kind of got into it, didn't we?" Will remarked.

"So what's next, Robb?" Jack asked.

Robb explained that the next step would be to validate the values by getting input from the entire company. As the chief executive, he said that he would send an email questionnaire to all employees explaining the process they had gone through and inviting comments and suggestions for additional values. He wanted to ensure that everyone had a chance to "buy in" to the values because they would need a broad support base if creating a values-based company culture was going to be successful.

Briefly, he outlined the next steps. The team would meet for two-hour sessions on Monday, Wednesday, and Friday for the next two weeks to build a strategy for aligning everything in the company around these core values.

Then they would work their way through the entire company, using ideas from employees at all levels, to create "values guidelines" for how the company would conduct business. These guidelines would clarify what values-based behaviors and decisions would be expected from all employees on a day-to-day basis.

"We will make our message crystal clear to everyone in the company: Whenever a person is faced with an action or with a decision, he or she will know how to use these values as a guide or a template. We will eliminate any ambiguity from what we expect of everyone at Central Plains Foods and motivate each person to pull together to reach our business goals. And we will have some great fun doing it!"

"How do you plan to do all that, Robb?"

"To be honest, I'm not 100 percent sure. But I'll know by Friday at 10:00 A.M. when we return to this conference room," he added, holding his index finger straight up in a confident oratory style.

Coach, I need you now!

～

Having Too Many Values

Is Like Serving too

Many Masters.

The Key Is Finding

Central Core Values to

Live By.

～

B

Involve everyone when the future's at stake,
and make very clear the directions to take.

～

ROBB WAS BEGINNING to feel like a regular at Henry's
Hot Dogs. After greeting Coach with his own version of
Coach's V-for-Victory wave, they sat on the same bench
and Robb described the meeting with his executive team.
As usual, Coach listened attentively and then began by
acknowledging Robb's efforts.

"First of all, Robb, you really did well! You took the
risk of introducing a whole new way of looking at your
company—the risk of being rejected, or maybe even
ridiculed. But you pulled it off because you truly believed
in what you were doing. Good job!" he said, patting Robb
on the shoulder.

Robb thanked Coach and noticed that the compliment
boosted his inner strength and commitment to get to the
next level of aligning his company.

"Now then," Coach began to probe, "where are you

going with this? Where do you want to end up?"

"What do you mean?"

"Well, why are you going to all this trouble focusing your company on values?"

Robb thought for a moment. "I'm doing it because I've come to believe that a common understanding and agreement about what's important is a solid way to run a team—or a company. And, partly I'm doing it because of the impact of that silly wake-up dream."

"What impact was that?" Coach asked.

"It shook me up a bit, Coach. Fear is too strong a word, but at some level I must have believed the company was unraveling a bit."

"What do you mean by unraveling?"

"In addition to some of the key business indicators, the place hasn't been feeling right. It was in the back of my mind, but I didn't pay attention to it. I guess it really didn't register until I had the dream."

Robb contemplated further. "Then I began to look around a little more carefully and noticed things like the survey results, Will's castigating approach to his sales rep, and Jack not holding the meeting he agreed to hold. And the fact that no one seemed to take our company values seriously. All of these things started to add up and give me an uncomfortable feeling."

"So the silly dream was . . . . " Coach paused.

" . . . maybe not so silly." Robb finished for him.

"There are many ways to get information, but one of the most reliable ways is to look inside. I'm not trying to psychologize, but I do think you must have been mulling these matters over in your mind, and that may have contributed to the dream. And, Good Buddy, you were smart enough to pay heed, or at least to check it out."

"The fact that the dream was about losing my job helped to get my attention—especially when I learned that there really is a special board meeting coming up," Robb admitted.

"Back to my earlier question: Where are you going with this? Where do you want to end up?"

"I want to end up with where I thought we were before all this happened—everyone in the company pulling together, living and working harmoniously and profitably."

"Based upon . . . " Coach prodded.

" . . . a commonly accepted set of core values." Robb finished Coach's sentence again.

"Right! Now you know where you want to be. By when?"

"Yesterday." Robb quipped.

"Not realistic. What *is* reasonable?" Coach asked.

"How about six months from now?" Robb offered.

"Reasonable. And how will you know that people in the company are, in fact, aligned with these values?"

"By how they act on the job—and presumably at

home and everywhere else."

"Okay. But how will all of your employees, individually, know how to act?" Coach continued.

"C'mon, Coach, if I give them the new set of values, explain that they came from the executive team and are validated by the whole company from my email survey, won't they know what's expected of them?" Robb asked plaintively.

"Not likely, Robb. Not very likely." Coach warned. "What you've done will go a long way, but it won't be enough. Let's get back to the meeting you held with the team. Tell me, what was behind the way you opened the meeting after everyone came back from the break?"

"I wanted them to understand how values influence behavior." Robb explained.

"What else?"

"I wanted them to be engaged in the learning process and to be part of what we were doing in our work session so they would buy in to the core values that we were identifying."

"Yep! And you exhibited a number of the core values in the way that you handled that meeting. You *communicated* your intentions clearly. You engaged the team in a new *learning* experience, and you went a long way toward gaining *trust* by admitting honestly that you were not exactly sure how you were going to make it all happen, but that you were very confident you would be ready by Friday. You did lots of things right in that session, Robb, according to the very set of values that were created. It was a great step forward toward establishing a values-based corporate culture."

Robb again accepted Coach's acknowledgement and felt increasingly confident that he would be able to figure out a strategy for embedding the core values throughout the company.

"Robb, how will you know when you've been successful in getting the employees to embrace the values you've established?" Coach asked.

"People will behave on the job in ways that are consistent with the values."

"Good. But how will they know what is expected of them?"

"I guess we'll have to communicate these expectations clearly." Robb answered as he began to think the process through.

"Do you know how you'll communicate with them?" Coach began to push for some specifics.

"I'm not sure yet. I think I'd like to get some ideas from the team."

"Excellent! But let's be sure we keep a couple of principles in mind as you create the process for getting buy-in from the troops." Coach continued, "What principle did you learn when you realized no one was paying attention to the company values that hang in twenty-seven locations around the office?"

"I learned that the values can't be pushed on them. They have to come from the people themselves—just like they did from the team in our last meeting—and the whole company needs to be involved in the process."

"Principle Number 1: Involve everyone in the creation of a set of values," Coach confirmed. "What else have you learned about this in the past couple of weeks?"

"A second principle I learned is that a statement of values is not enough. What I mean is, let's take the value of *respect*—the one that got more votes than any other value in our meeting. My people don't always act respectfully. They don't always do what they say. They 'talk the talk' but they don't 'walk the walk.'

"For example, I noted that both Jack and Will voted for respect, but yet, in my view, Jack didn't respect his colleagues when he failed to conduct the brainstorm session with his people. And Will didn't treat his sales rep respectfully. If they thought about it, I bet they'd realize that they were behaving out of sync with their own values."

"So what's the principle you need to keep in mind?" Coach asked.

"Specific expectations must be clear. Behaviors that are acceptable and consistent with our values—and, likewise, those actions that are *not* consistent with our values—need to be communicated."

"You've got it," Coach confirmed again, *"Principle Number 2: Expectations must be communicated clearly."*

"Now, what's the third big lesson, or principle, you've learned recently?"

"I don't know, Coach. I'm not sure there is a third principle," Robb answered.

"If you did learn a third principle, what would it be?" Coach teased.

Robb was thoughtful for a moment. "Okay, you're right. It's obvious. *Encouragement.* When you notice people doing the right thing, you let them know it—you reinforce them. This gets into the whole notion of rewards and recognition."

"So . . . what is the third principle?" Coach wanted the words to come from Robb.

"Principle Number 3: Monitor and reward the right behaviors."

Coach and Robb continued for over an hour. Coach asked questions, Robb responded. If the answer he came up with didn't seem satisfactory, Coach would take another tack, always probing to help Robb clarify what he already knew but had not taken the time to think through completely.

At the end of their time together, Coach remarked that he thought Robb had many more of the answers in him than he realized and added, "I think you're on the right track, Robb. Now the challenge will be to see how your executive team and the rest of the employees respond to the plan you've just laid out."

"That *we've* just laid out," Robb corrected him.

"No, not really. I haven't come up with one idea this afternoon about what to do next. They've all come from you. All I did was to ask questions—you came up with the ideas.

The entire plan you've just outlined is yours. The challenge now is to get your executive team behind you and make sure your plan is understood by everyone. When you've got 'em all behind you, you will be able to implement your program effectively. I think you are going to do fine, Robb. Be sure to let me know how it goes."

With that, Coach bid farewell and waved his trademark two-fingered V as he walked away. Robb sat on the bench a while longer building his strategy for getting company-wide support for the new set of core values.

Three Principles Guide

Values-Based Leadership:

Involve Everyone;

Communicate Expectations Clearly; and

Reward Behaviors that

Reflect the

Core Values of the Organization.

14

*Preach good words, if you must
but how you act is what we'll trust.*

≈

ON FRIDAY, AT 10:00 A.M., everyone was gathered in the conference room and ready to go—except Jack, that is. Robb inquired, but no one seemed to know where Jack was. It was not lost on most of the rest of the team that Jack was frequently late. His meetings rarely started on time. People had just come to accept that Jack was a busy guy as the COO, and that he needed to be cut a bit of slack.

Mary suggested that the team get started without him and a couple of others agreed, including Robb. He began the meeting by sharing the results of the validation survey that he conducted.

"You all saw the email questionnaire that I sent to everyone in the company. I was pleased that over 90 percent of the employees responded within twenty-four hours, almost all of them positive and appreciative that we asked for their input. And, a significant number of folks responded to my invitation to add new values. Almost all of those people requested that we add the value of *honesty* to the list. So, with your permission, I'd like to expand our list to six core values: *Customer Satisfaction, Trust, Communication, Learning, Respect, and Honesty.*"

There was unanimous agreement and everyone was eager and attentive as Robb moved on. He continued by introducing the principles he developed with Coach. Instead of three, however, he was prepared to introduce four. After he thought about how to implement the core values, it occurred to him that introducing a new way of thinking and acting throughout the company was a big deal. It would be important for all employees to have a clear understanding of what was expected of them and why. To be successful in the new environment they were creating, everyone would need to have the context and the rationale that Robb and the executive team had created.

Simply stated, everyone in the company deserved to know where the company was going and what the plan was for getting there. Hence, a new principle: *Create a compelling vision of the future.*

"Remember the paradigm I drew on the board last time?" Robb asked. Everyone nodded as Robb drew the diagram and explained once again how values are behind the beliefs and attitudes that drive behavior.

"Well, I've done a little more thinking and I've added another element," he said as he passed out a sheet with an additional box in the diagram.

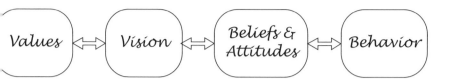

"Our values also influence our vision of where we want to take this company. Another way of saying it is that our vision must be consistent with our values if we are going to be true to ourselves, our employees, our customers, and our stockholders.

Robb went on to explain the rationale behind his thinking. "Values—those concepts we hold dear, those things that are important to us—form the foundation for how we do things around here. *How we do things around here* defines who we are as a company and what we stand for. It is the basis of our culture at Central Plains.

"Our vision" he continued, "communicates who we are and what we do. Our vision is our rallying flag; it provides a clear picture of where we are going. It tells our story to everyone inside and outside the company," Robb offered. "Anyone care to explain how beliefs and attitudes fit into this corporate culture paradigm?"

"Sure." It was Danielle. "I see this from my perspective as CFO. Our country is being rocked by financial scandals of major proportion and we are still reeling from the effects. Companies overstate revenues by billions to raise stock prices and use questionable, even illegal, accounting principles. Firms collapse. We're having a moral crisis with worldwide impact. Confidence in the market has suffered and people are wary. Much of the ongoing crisis, it seems to me, happens because of a casual attitude toward values, or the leadership doesn't believe in having a strong set of ethical values in the first place," she concluded.

"So, the beliefs and attitudes element in this paradigm form the framework for the company," Wanda added. "Not only do our employees need to understand where we're going and how we're going to get there, but they must also know why our company behaves as a whole the way it does. And that can be understood only in the context of our values."

Brett chimed in. "There are always a lot of jokes about us lawyers and our questionable values. But, to be fair, we have a very strong commitment to an ethical code of conduct. What I see here is a real opportunity to use this diagram as a way for any company or professional firm to help communicate and set the standards for ethically-based, values-driven behavior."

"Right, Brett," Mark Peavey added, "if we can rally all of our people to get behind a core set of values and understand how these values help to determine where the company is going and how it's going to get there, it should be easy for them to shape up their attitudes and get with the program."

The discussion became so engaging that no one

noticed when Jack came into the room. He began to offer
an apology, but his voice trailed off when he realized that
it didn't seem as though he'd been missed.

"*Attitudes*," Robb focused the discussion, "determine
what we do. Therefore, it's easy to see by working backward through this paradigm, that the way we do things
around here, that is, our culture, is derived directly from
our *vision*. Vision defines where we are going. And, all of
it ties right back into our foundation of *values*—those
things we think are important."

Robb paused and Jack jumped in with, "It looks like
you guys have really been going at it. What have you
been talking about?"

"Too late, Jack, you should know that if you drop your
pencil in this class, it's like missing half a semester!" Will
quipped and drew a couple of supporting smiles.

With that, Robb suggested a five-minute break.

❧

Vision Defines

Where We Are Going.

It Reflects Our Values.

Together, Vision and Values

Shape Our Attitudes.

Our Attitudes Determine

What We Do.

❧

15

*The best ideas come from teams that trust,
because no **one** of us is as smart as **all** of us.*

JACK CAUGHT UP with Robb in the hall during the break and began to give an excuse for why he was late. Robb interrupted him with, "Jack, I'm glad you're here. Your input is important to this process. We have a lot to do, so let's finish up the meeting, and you and I can take a few minutes after it's over to talk about whatever else is on your mind, okay?"

"Sure, Robb. I'll come to your office after the meeting."

"See you then," Robb replied.

Robb began the second half of the meeting. "Up to now this has all been academic. Our real challenge is to figure out how to *implement* this values-based culture throughout the company.

"Implementation is everything. Throughout our careers, we've all seen initiatives that have failed. Most of the time, the failure has nothing to do with how good the ideas were or how important the initiative was. They fail because they are not implemented well. The best ideas in the world can sit on a shelf and collect dust.

"In our case, if our employees don't buy into our values-based culture, we won't have one," Robb explained. Then he added, "Team, I can't figure this one out on my own. I really need your help."

"You got it, Boss. I'll help in any way that I can." Will offered. "How about the rest of you?"

"Of course."

"I'm in."

There was a chorus of supporting comments.

"Thanks everyone, I really appreciate your positive attitude about this. Here's what we've got so far: a set of four principles that I believe can guide our implementation plan. Let me restate them for you, and then we can brainstorm and come up with a go-forward strategy."

Robb peeled back the pages of the flip chart and uncovered a page on which he had written his four principles:

Implementation Principles

1. Involve everyone in the creation of a set of values.
2. Create a compelling vision of the future.
3. Communicate expectations clearly.
4. Monitor and reward the right behaviors.

After reading the principles aloud and giving the team a few minutes to think about them, Robb enlisted their help. They spent time interpreting their meaning, why they were important, and in the process, they created a strong sense of ownership for each of them. Robb then explained that he wanted their best thinking about how each principle would impact their implementation plan.

A number of good ideas were generated. Then Alicia came up with a suggestion. "This is a little overwhelming. Would it make sense if we divided up the four principles and came back with recommendations at our next meeting?"

Everyone liked the idea and Robb agreed. "Excellent suggestion, Alicia. Who wants to work on each of these principles?"

Four teams were formed. Alicia and Brett volunteered to think through the third principle and come up with a communications plan for implementing the values initiative.

Mary and Jack wanted to work on the fourth principle, monitoring and rewarding behaviors.

Wanda and Danielle offered to take on the vision statement, adding that they would begin by reviewing the company's current marketing materials. Robb, noting they didn't have a vision statement, asked to join their team.

Finally, the challenge of getting everyone in the company involved in the process so they would support the new core values was assigned to Mark and Will.

"I think that's the toughest one of all, and the two of you are clearly the best qualified to handle it," Robb encouraged. Others agreed that Will's marketing genius and customer knowledge plus Mark's understanding of front-line employees made them the right team to work on the implementation principle.

"There you have it, Team. Put your best thoughts on paper, and be ready to present your case on Wednesday morning. Because this is the real meat of our planning, I want to take a full half-day for the next session. See you all here at 8:00 A.M. sharp!"

Jack winced, but no one seemed to notice.

❧

Implementation

Is Everything!

16

*A crisis in values that hits first at home
will doggedly follow wherever you roam.*

JACK DID NOT COME to Robb's office after the meeting. Instead, he called and asked if he could come by the next morning. He said that he had a little soul searching to do and he wanted to sleep on it before he met with Robb. Robb agreed to the request and put Jack on his calendar for 8:30 A.M. the next day.

At home that evening, Robb talked with Sharon about Jack's half-hearted team effort. Her instincts were cued immediately and she counseled Robb that those seemed like telltale signs of personal distress. She was concerned and hoped that Jack was not in any serious personal crisis.

Jack was waiting in Robb's office when he came in at 8:15 that morning. He was uncharacteristically a bit edgy. Jack always had a great deal of confidence and acted very sure of himself. Robb noted Jack's discomfort as they sat down at the round meeting table.

"Want a coffee or a water, Jack?"

"No, thanks, Robb. I'm fine."

Robb waited.

"I see you're not going to make this easy," Jack started.

"No reason for it to be hard."

"Actually, there is."

It was Robb's turn to get a little uncomfortable.

"What do you mean?"

"Well, after yesterday's session, I started to take a hard look at my commitment to the company. Until yesterday, I treated these value sessions pretty much like any other corporate exercise—as something that I could do with 10 percent of my energy and focus."

"You mean you've only been giving me 10 percent of your talent?" Robb tried to lighten the conversation a little.

"You know what I mean. I can usually handle multiple tasks simultaneously. It's one of the reasons you and I both agreed that the COO role is a good one for me. But, to be honest, I've let it get a little out of hand. I had come to believe that I could handle as much as anyone could throw at me. But, you know what? I can't." He paused.

"So what are you telling me, Jack?" Robb asked, now concerned for his colleague.

"This is a little tough for me, Robb, so I ask that you please keep it between us."

"Absolutely."

"I've gotten involved with so many things both at the

office and in my personal life that I'm overwhelmed. I did-
n't realize it until we began this values exercise, and it
really came home to me when I walked into the meeting
yesterday, late, and I realized that I wasn't part of the team.

"That distressed me. So after the meeting, I thought a
lot about the values we created—not just the six core values—but all thirty-two or thirty-four of them. At first I
focused on the ones that I think I've really been living:
excellence, success, confidence, and profitability. Those
seemed fine until I realized that they were all to satisfy
my own personal needs. I wanted top ratings on all of
those things for my own selfish benefit and reward."

Robb waited. "And . . . . "

"And the problem is that I'd lost sight of some other
values that are important to me, like, *teamwork, balance,
reliability, kindness, humor, fun*—but most of all, *family.*

"Robb, I've gotten so caught up in the personal investing and trading and working on some 'big idea' start-up
ventures, that I'm hardly home in the evenings. Or when I
am there, I'm on my computer until the wee hours. The
result is not only that I've been getting into the office later
than I should, but I don't know what my kids are up to,
and I can't remember the last time I had an intimate conversation with Lynne, much less a romantic night out."

"Have you talked with Lynne about this? Robb asked
gently.

"Finally. Yesterday after our meeting, I really stewed

about this. I was a little angry, feeling like I was being left out and then forced by the team to conform to a new set of standards. I actually began to consider if I should leave the company. By late afternoon, I felt pretty alone and depressed. Part of the result of being spread so thin is that I've begun to make some poor decisions in the market, and I lost pretty big on some investments." He paused in reflection.

"As the afternoon wore on, I found myself staring at the walls. I finally realized that I've become so worried that I'm driving myself to distraction. I sat there feeling like a train wreck about to happen."

"Why do you think you felt that way?" Robb probed gently.

"Well, believe it or not, Robb, I think it's because I've been out of sync with my own values. I'd simply gotten caught up with everything, thinking mostly about success and forgetting some of the other values that are very important to me. At that moment yesterday afternoon I decided to do something about it."

"What did you do?"

"I called Lynne to tell her that I was on my way and wanted to spend some time with her before dinner. She wasn't home. That was unusual at 4:30 in the afternoon. But I didn't think too much about it until I was almost home and I realized that I was wondering anxiously where she could be. I found myself getting a little worked up and actually driving too fast to get home."

"When I got there, her car was in the garage, and I felt a physical sense of relief. But then I wondered why she didn't answer the phone and if she had been home all along. Was she unable to get to it? Robb, I worked myself into a real state of anxiety until I went in and found Lynne in the kitchen. I almost collapsed when I saw she was fine. Lynne looked at me, surprised, and said 'You're home early! What's the occasion?'"

"What did you say?" Robb wondered.

"I was a little nonplussed. I felt foolish getting so worked up, but I realized it was partly because I'd been so stressed and worried lately. Mostly, though, I had a real epiphany about just how much I love Lynne and the kids and how devastated I would be without them. So I went over and hugged her and told her how important she was to me and how sorry I was that I'd been so self-absorbed and unavailable in the past months."

"Then that's a good thing." Robb said.

"Oh, yeah, but you haven't heard the worst part."

Robb braced himself, and Jack went on.

"Lynne said that she had just come home from an afternoon coffee with her best friend, Phyllis. She wanted some advice from Phyllis because she was at her wits' end, feeling our marriage was failing, and we were slipping apart. Then she started to cry. Robb, she told me she was thinking of leaving me."

There was fear and pain in Jack's eyes.

Robb was initially surprised and sympathized with him. Then he began to fit the pieces of the puzzle together and a lot of the issues around Jack began to make sense. He was in crisis.

"Jack, how can I help?"

"Actually, just letting me get this off my chest is helping a lot. Lynne and I talked for a long time last night and agreed that it made a lot more sense to spend money on a good marriage counselor than on a divorce lawyer."

"Smart."

"Do you know how to find one?"

"Actually, I do. Mary has a list of highly qualified counselors as part of our HR referral network. I'll call and get some names for you. And don't worry, I won't tell her who asked. This is strictly confidential," Robb assured him.

"Thanks. Another thing is that I want you to know that I'm rededicating myself to Central Plains' business, and I hope you'll have a little patience with me as I reset my priorities. I want to stay here and help the team take the company to the next level."

"Your leaving the company is not an option," Robb stated matter-of-factly, leaving no doubt of his support for Jack. "What else can I do?"

"Keep my feet to the fire on this values initiative. It's important to me and to the company, and I really want to do my part to make the implementation a success."

"Done. Anything else?"

"Not that I can think of."

"Good. Now get out of here and get to work with Mary on how we're going to monitor and reward the right work behaviors around here," Robb chided and playfully punched him on the shoulder, reminding Jack that he and Mary had a team assignment.

⚉

You Are the Same Person at

Home, at Work, and at Play.

You Take You—and Your Values—

With You Wherever You Go.

⚉

17

*Share the work, share the play,
and celebrate often along the way!*

IT WAS REMARKABLE. An incredible amount of work
and solid thinking had taken place since the last work
session. Robb let everyone know how pleased he was
with the implementation planning.

Wanda, Danielle, and Robb kicked off the meeting.
They explained how they evaluated all of the company
marketing materials using the core values as a tool.
Without bothering to go back to rewrite any of the old
material, they said they wanted the team to create a new
Values-Based Vision of the Future together.

Wanda explained. "Our *Vision* is about where we are
going. It is our lofty ideal. JFK said it best with his vision
for the space race in the early 1960s:

*I believe this nation should commit itself, to achieving
the goal, before this decade is out, of landing a man on
the moon and returning him safely to the earth.*

"This vision was so powerful that it outlived Kennedy by six years when Neil Armstrong set foot on the moon in 1969. Inspired by this historically significant vision, we set out to have a vision for Central Plains that is equally inspiring in our own way."

"And notice," Danielle added, "that our ideas for our vision have the same elements of this famous moon statement: it indicates clearly what we will achieve, by when, and how we will measure our success."

The whole team went to work and, based on the research and thinking of Wanda and Danielle, it didn't take long to agree upon an acceptable first draft:

In five years, Central Plains Foods will have sixty million dollars in revenues and will have been awarded the Midwest Food Distribution Association's "Number 1 in Service Excellence Award" for five years in a row.

Because they had already won the award the last two years running, all they had to do would be to keep up the good work and grow the business!

Mark and Will were eager to go next. They were not content with a "chalk talk," so they created an animated computer presentation that demonstrated some of the multimedia communication techniques that the marketing department had devised.

It was brilliant! With Mark's sensitivity to the front-line employees and Will's humor, they came up with a clever way to extend the values and vision of the company via the company Intranet. Most important, they explained, was the opportunity to involve the employees in defining how the company values could help to define job behaviors and job evaluation procedures.

The whole team was convinced that Will and Mark had come up with a great strategy for giving everyone a true sense of involvement in developing the company culture.

Alicia and Brett challenged the team to critique their communication plan matrix with its three dimensions: messages, audiences, and communication channels. They had thoroughly reviewed who needed to know about Central Plains' values, vision, and mission, and concluded that there were five major audiences: customers, employees, shareowners, the food services industry, and the general public.

For each of these groups, Alicia and Brett identified what each audience would be interested in, what they would need to know, what actions they wanted each group to take as a result of getting the communications, and what would be the best way to get the messages to them. They considered everything from voicemail and email, to public relations, to advertising, and laid out a plan of action over the next six months with clear accountabilities and deadlines for systematic implementation.

The team brainstormed additional messages for employees, customers, and potential customers, some of which were hilarious, and others that would clearly never leave the room!

Finally, Jack and Mary presented a reward and recognition system that dovetailed with the work that had been presented by the others. In addition to building the value statements into a new job description format that would make the company values crystal clear to every employee, they created a huge wall poster entitled, *"How We Do Things Around Here—and Why"* And with that, the culture of the company was clearly defined.

The poster listed and defined the new core values (Jack and Mary acknowledged they could change with Will and Mark's survey results). In addition, they took each of the major areas of the business—for example, customer service, accounts receivable, warehousing, and so forth, and listed the job classifications of people who worked in those areas. Then they provided specific examples of the "Central Plains' Way" of behaving in each area. One included appropriate ways for delivery personnel to interface with customers that would demonstrate the values of *trust* and *respect.*

By noon, the team was exhausted but playfully happy. They had not only outlined a comprehensive *Values Initiative Implementation Plan,* but they had fun doing it. And all along, they demonstrated each of their core values of trust, respect, customer satisfaction, communication, honesty, and learning.

"Before we end today, let's recognize one additional

value: *celebration!*" Robb announced. "Lunch is on me at the golf club. See you there at 12:30."

Before heading out for lunch, Robb stopped in his office. He was positively brimming with excitement. He grabbed the phone and punched in some numbers. After a couple of rings and a hello, Robb spoke into the mouthpiece, "Coach, I can't wait to tell you what just happened. You're not going to believe it!"

❧

Set Expectations,

Inspire the Team . . . and

Celebrate Success!

18

*We'll never know if the nightmare was real
or if dreams of sleep have truth to reveal.*

THE PHONE CALL from the chairman came a few days later. "Robb, I imagine you're chomping at the bit to discuss the agenda for our special board of directors' meeting next Tuesday."

"Well, I *have* been wondering about the agenda, Dr. Anderson."

"How about we meet for lunch today? I want to let you know what's been concerning me lately. If you don't mind, I'd like to have lunch at a special place that you might enjoy . . . ."

An hour later, Robb and Chairman Anderson were finishing up their sandwiches sitting on the bench next to Henry's Hot Dogs. Dr. Anderson had just confided, with apologies, that he had decided to drop in and chat informally with some of the employees at Central Plains during the past few weeks. Using his charm, he said, chuckling modestly, he was able to persuade some folks to let him in on the buzz of enthusiasm among the troops about the new *Values Initiative*.

"Therefore, based on what I hear, Robb, I don't think we need to have a special board meeting after all. The executive committee of the board of directors was going to put a merger proposal on the table. And the numbers looked pretty good. But after looking into both companies a little further, it was clear to me that the values of the two organizations don't mesh at all, and we would be setting ourselves up for a difficult post merger culture clash. Our values of 'customers first' and 'learning' do not blend well with 'profitability, speed, and efficiency,' the driving values of the other company. I discussed this with the committee members, and the merger is off."

As that announcement hung in the air, both men were interrupted by a friendly shout, "Good afternoon, Gentlemen!"

They looked up to see Coach as he walked by with his characteristic victory wave, his twinkling eyes above his snow-white beard, and a smile.

"Hi, Coach!" Both men greeted him simultaneously, then looked at each other with an unspoken question hanging in the air, *"How do you know Coach Olson?"*

The chairman broke the silence. "Say, Robb, did I ever tell you that I was on a championship soccer team at Vicksburg State back in the early 80s ...."

It is True that

"No Man Is an Island."

Winners Always Have

Others Who Have

Helped Them

Along the Way.

Acknowledgements

THANKS TO THE many colleagues, friends, and family who encouraged me to write this book.

Some special teams have lent extraordinary support. Many thanks to:

The San Diego Chairs of The Executive Committee (TEC) who held me accountable for including the book in my personal strategic plan.

The CEOs in TEC 86 who reviewed the first manuscript draft and, in the words of one somewhat surprised member, said "Hey, this is really good!"

The members of Dr. Tom Hill's Eagle Institute who have joined *The Values-Based Revolution—a Movement to Recover Our Personal Ideals.*

Dean Curtis Cook's team including Jerry Singleton, Dave Wyman, and Mark Divine for providing a model of a values-based organization at the *Leadership Institute for Entrepreneurs* (LIFE) at the University of San Diego.

And thanks to these special few who stand out as being exceptionally encouraging:

Boaz Rauchwerger and his indefatigable belief in me and faith in my writing.

Ed Sternagle, whose enthusiasm made me consider making him my agent after he read the first draft.

Orienne Strode and Bill Maloney, inspirational teachers who have taught me so much about living a values-based life.

Carter McClelland, whose touching reaction to the story touched me.

Jeff Glenn-Levin, who has stuck with me through thick and thin with advice, counsel, and loving critique.

Carmel Myers, whose condensed version of Aristotle is part of the inspiration for the concept of values-based leadership: *You are what you do.*

Mort Shaevitz, who taught me the value of coaches having coaches.

John Cotter for his suggestion that every TEC member and TEC Chair could learn from this story.

Claude Alverson, whose creative genius never ceases to amaze me.

John Assaraf, who has been my pulling guard sharing his knowledge as he broke ground in uncharted territory.

Gail Kearns, my book shepherd, and her team,

Peri Poloni and Lucy Levenson, who are still guiding me along the path of authorship with editing, design, and strategy.

Michael Kaplan, who is inspirational and encouraging by his nature.

And to my wife, Lynette, who has had faith in me for these so many years and to our "kids" Annie and Joey who *arf* and *meow* their approval and support on a daily basis.

❧

About the Author

A FORMER COLLEGE PROFESSOR and successful management consultant, Ken Majer's key focus today is to encourage as many business and government leaders as he can to join what he calls The Values-Based Revolution—A Movement to Recover Our Personal Ideals. This book, *Values-Based Leadership: A Revolutionary Approach to Business Success and Personal Prosperity,* is the first of a series of books that he is writing on the topic of restoring positive and productive principles in one's personal and professional life.

Majer shares his values-based leadership messages through his writing, speaking, seminars, and workshops. In addition, a growing series of values-based leadership products are being released. Please go to

www.majervalues.com

or call 877-958-2583 toll-free for more information about

Keynote Addresses

45-60 Minute Presentations

Half-day Executive Seminars

Full-day Management Workshops

Strategic Implementation Programs

Values-Based Leadership Audio Books

Values-Based Leadership CD Learning Programs

Quick Order Form

Online orders:	www.majervalues.com
Fax orders:	858-552-4479
Telephone orders:	877-958-2583 toll free
Email orders:	orders@majervalues.com
Postal orders:	MajerCommunications
	3655 Nobel Drive, Suite 160
	San Diego, California 92122-1004

❧

I would like to order _____ copies of *Values-Based Leadership*
@ \$26.00 each. *(For quantity discounts and special sales please
go to orders at www.majervalues.com)*

Name: _____

Address:_____

City:_____

State: _____ Zip: _____

Telephone:_____ Email address: _____

Sales tax: CA residents please add 7.75%.

Shipping by air:
US: \$4.00 for the first book and \$2.00 for each additional book.
International: \$9.00 for the first book and \$5.00 for each additional book (estimate)

Payment: ☐ Check—Make checks payable to MajerStrategies, Inc.

☐ Visa   ☐ MasterCard   ☐ Discover   ☐ American Express

Card number: _____

Name as it appears on card: _____ Exp. date: _____

Name: _____

Address where credit card statement is sent: _____

City: _____ State: _____ Zip _____

For more information on Dr. Ken Majer's seminars and
presentations, please go to the website at
www.majervalues.com or call toll free 877-958-2583

THANK YOU FOR YOUR ORDER!

MajerCommunicati